The Little Manger Mouse

by Phyllis Didleau
Illustrated by Gretchen Gackstatter

The Little Manger Mouse
Second edition, August 1, 2021. Previously published by Mother's House Publishing, Inc.
Original illustrations in watercolor by Gretchen Gackstatter

Published by BOOK BOOK SQUARED
P.O. Box 60144
Colorado Springs, Colorado 80960

Printed in the United States of America

ISBN 978-1-943829-37-8

www.goldenrulemasterpieces.com
www.mangermouse.com

BOOK BOOK SQUARED is an imprint of Rhyolite Press, LLC

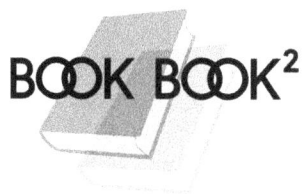

BOOK BOOK²

To the Lord
And His Great Commission
And he said unto them,
Go ye into the world and preach
the gospel to every creature.
Mark 16:15 KJV

Over 2000 years ago
a family of mice lived in a manger
in the little town of Bethlehem.

On one special warm evening
the cattle were lowing with contentment.
The sheep and donkey lay around the straw and a
couple of goats joined the little group of animals.
Huddled together, the animals were a picture
of peace and joy.

Just as the herd was settling in for the night
and sleep was upon them, the sound of
human footsteps and voices broke
the silence of the evening.

"Be quiet," Father Mouse said to his Wife Mouse. "There are humans about the stable." He was especially protective of his wife because she was expecting the arrival of several baby mice at any moment.

Father Mouse scampered quickly back into his nest, making sure none of the footsteps were upon him. This was their first family event and they were very excited because they were sure this night would bring special joy into their lives.

"This will be fine," Father Mouse heard the voice of a young man exclaim. "There is no room in the Inn but this is warm and dry, a wonderful place for my wife and me to spend the night. Besides, the animals will be of great comfort to us and the open stable will let the light of the bright star in the east shine down upon us."

Making a soft bed for his wife, he made sure
she was warm and comfortable for she, too, was
expecting an event of great joy during the night.

By morning, history
had been changed.

For there in the stable, a little mouse family, themselves delighted by the arrival of their first baby mice, witnessed the Greatest Event in Humankind.

As the joy of new life came to their family, so new life was also presented to the world through the birth of a little baby boy named Jesus, son of God and Mary and Joseph.

Father Mouse was humbled. "Why, oh, why was I chosen to witness this event?" Deep down in his heart he knew the answer.

"I was chosen because I can carry the message of this night and scamper throughout the city telling everyone of the occasion and no one will give me credit so I cannot become prideful. That is the way God would want it. So I must tell the story. It is my responsibility, since I know the story."

"That is the way God would want it."

"I must tell all I saw and heard. I must spread the Good News."

This little mouse you see here is to remind you that you, too, have been chosen to tell the story. You must tell everyone about The Great Event in Bethlehem. You must tell the story that the little manger mouse told.

You must!!

The Little Manger Mouse

Children's Mini-Drama
for ages 3-8
for home, school,
and church

The Little Manger Mouse
Children's Mini-Drama for ages 3-8
for home, school, and church

Teach performance skills and encourage evangelism by:
  a. learning to understand stage layout
  b. acquiring beginning skills in voice projection
  c. developing listening skills and following directions
  d. assisting memorization
  e. explaining the importance of telling others about Jesus

There are three presentation models from which to choose so that every budget and group size can be included.
  a. Basic: A reader reads the story and characters walk through the actions with only signs tied around their neck to indicate the part they are playing.
  b. Enhanced: A reader narrates the story and the characters memorize the parts. Simple costumes.
  c. Professional: Reader and memorized parts plus music, microphones, curtains, and complete costumes.

Stage:
A raised platform is most desirable. However, if a complete stage area with exits, entries, curtains and lights is not available, do not hesitate to use facilities that are available. A room with an audience is all that is really needed. If presenting to other children, the audience can sit on the floor.

Characters: (minimum 6):
Father Manger Mouse
Mother Manger Mouse
Reader (older child or adult)
Baby manger mice 1,2,3,4, or more
Joseph
Mary
Baby Jesus (doll)
Animals: donkey, sheep, goats, duck, chicken, cow

Support:
Sound Effects Coordinator
Light Coordinator

Carol:
Lyrics may be provided to the audience for their participation if desired. You may wish to limit each carol to one verse.

Costumes:
These can be very simple or very elaborate depending on the available adult participation for help. If help is limited, a simple sign on each character around the neck will suffice. Write on the sign "Father Mouse", "Sheep" etc. Brown paper bags with eye holes and simple faces drawn with markers would be all you need or perhaps a make-up artist could transform their faces with face paint.

Sound:
Tapes can be used or a Youth Choir or other group can sing the carols.

Stage Setting:
The drama takes place in one act: the stable. On stage in the stable, the manger is right of center stage. Father and Mother Mouse peek out from under the manger.

The Play:

Reader: (spot light on reader) Over 2000 years ago a family of mice lived in a manger in the little town of Bethlehem.

Music: O Little Town of Bethlehem

Reader: On one special, warm evening, the cattle were lowing with contentment.

Sound Effects: Cattle lowing ("moo, moo" softly)

Reader: The sheep and donkey lay around the straw and a couple of goats joined the little group of animals. Huddled together, the animals were a picture of peace and joy.

Action: Sheep and donkey first, then the rest of the animals move closer together

Reader: Just as the herd was settling in for the night and sleep was upon them…

Action: Animals close eyes

Reader: The sound of human footsteps…

Sound Effects: Stomp, stomp, stomp

Reader: and voices…

Sound Effects: Voices mumbling

Reader: broke the silence of the evening.

Father Mouse: (kindly) Shh! There are humans about the stable!

Action: Leaves manger area to peek out the door, puts finger to lips and looks at wife mouse. Holds hand up to indicate that she stay in place.

Reader: He was especially protective of his wife because she was expecting the arrival of several baby mice any moment.

Action: Father Mouse puts his arm around Mother Mouse, who smiles as she pats her plump tummy.

Reader: Father Mouse scampered quickly back into the nest with his wife, making sure none of the footsteps were upon them.

Action:	Father Mouse and Mother Mouse scamper back to manger from near the door.
Joseph:	(from outside door) This will be fine. There is no room in the inn but this is warm and dry, a wonderful place for my wife and me to spend the night.
Action:	Joseph enters the stable—looks around, and waves hand over area.
Joseph:	(pointing to animals) Besides, the animals will be of great comfort to us and the open stable will let the light of the bright star (points to star) in the east shine down upon us.
Reader:	Making a soft straw bed for his wife, Joseph made sure she was warm and comfortable, for she, too, was expecting an event of great joy during the night.
Action:	Joseph makes a bed and covers her with a blanket.
Music:	It Came Upon a Midnight Clear
Reader:	By morning, history had been changed. For there in the stable a little mouse family, themselves delighted by the arrival of their first baby mice, witnessed the Greatest Event in all humankind.
Action:	Joseph and Mary look upon their baby, Jesus.

Music:	Joy To The World
Reader:	For as the joy of new life came to their family, so new life was also presented to the world through the birth of a little baby boy named Jesus, son of God, Mary and Joseph. Father Mouse was humbled.
Father Mouse:	Why, oh, why, was I chosen to witness this event?
Reader:	Deep down in his heart, he knew the answer.
Father Mouse:	I was chosen because I can carry the message of this night and scamper throughout the city telling everyone of the occasion and no one will give me credit so I cannot become prideful. That is the way God would want it. So I must tell the story. It is my responsibility since I know the story. That is the way God would want it. I must tell all I saw and heard. I must spread the Good News.
Music:	Go Tell It On The Mountain
Reader:	This little mouse you see here is to remind you that you, too, have been chosen to tell the story. You must tell everyone about the Great Event in Bethlehem. You must tell the story that the little manger mouse told. You must!
Music:	Hark The Herald Angels Sing

The End

Christmas Carol Lyrics

To download complete lyrics visit www.mangermouse.com

It Came Upon A Midnight Clear

It came upon the midnight clear,
That glorious song of old,
From angels bending near the earth,
To touch their harps of gold:
"Peace on the earth, goodwill to men,
From heaven's all gracious King!"
The world in solemn stillness lay
To hear the angels sing.

Go Tell It On The Mountain

While shepherds kept their watching
O'er silent flocks by night,
Behold throughout the heavens
There shone a holy light.

Go, tell it on the mountain,
Over the hills and everywhere,
Go, tell it on the mountain,
That Jesus Christ is born.

Oh Little Town Of Bethlehem

Oh little town of Bethlehem,
How still we see thee lie!
Above thy deep and dreamless sleep
The silent stars go by;
Yet in thy dark streets shineth,
The everlasting light;
The hopes and fears of all the years
Are met in thee tonight.

Joy To The World

Joy to the world! The Lord is come!
Let earth receive her King;
Let every heart prepare Him room,
And Heaven and nature sing,
And Heaven and nature sing,
And Heaven and Heaven and nature sing.

Hark The Herald Angels Sing

Hark the herald angels sing,
"Glory to the newborn King!"
Peace on earth and mercy mild,
God and sinners reconciled"
Joyful, all ye nations rise
Join the triumph of the skies;
With angelic host proclaim,
"Christ is born in Bethlehem"
Hark! The herald angels sing,
"Glory to the new-born King!"

The author, Phyllis Constant Didleau, holds a Bachelor Degree with a Life Certificate in elementary education from the University of Northern Colorado in Greeley. As a postgraduate student, she studied in Special Education at the University of Hawaii in Honolulu. Phyllis has many years experience in the classroom.

As a high school student she taught Sunday School and has been the Director of Children's Church. She has provided years of volunteering teaching children and participating in Vacation Bible School. Her Biblical studies include a two-year course from the Institute of Theology by Extension through the Department of International Studies, Open Bible Churches.

Gretchen Gackstatter, the illustrator, received a Bachelor Degree in Fine Arts from the University of Northern Colorado, Greeley. Over the years, she has taught art from kindergarten through high school. At the present time she teaches watercolor at the Argonne Gallery in St. Louis, Missouri. Her watercolors have gained a wide, popular reputation.

www.ingramcontent.com/pod-product-compliance
Lightning Source LLC
LaVergne TN
LVHW070840080426
835512LV00025B/3488